A Christian 12 Step Recovery Program

By

Joseph Kearney

©Copyright 2019 by Joseph Kearney All rights reserved.

This book is printed in the United States of America.

ISBN 978-0-578-00256-9

This Book is dedicated to my Mother and Father. Thank you, Dad, for teaching me the power of forgiveness. Thank you, Mom, for teaching me that character does matter and always being there for me.

Acknowledgments

I want to thank the following people for making my life and this work possible. My Aunt Rita, a Catholic Sister of IHM, who always prayed for me.

Father Joe C. who was there at 3 a.m. for my mother when my father died and he remains a friend to this day. Andy G. for helping to save my life, Andy A. for taking me through the Steps. And the following who either went through the Steps with me or worked on them in some fashion. Neal P. Cliff S. Marjorie S. K.K. Linda G. Rosemary F. Gerry F. Linda M. Melanie C. Teresa M. Roger N. Teresa B. Gene W. Pastor Berg. " I thank my God upon every remembrance of you". Philippians 1:3

CONTENTS

Introduction

9

Chapter One

The Twelve Step Recovery Program

12

Chapter Two

The Journey

15

Chapter Three

Step One

20

Chapter Four

Step Two

23

Chapter Five

Step Three

25

Chapter Six

Step Four

28

Chapter Seven

Step Five

38

Chapter Eight

Step Six

39

Chapter Nine

Step Seven

40

Chapter Ten

Step Eight

41

Chapter Eleven

Step Nine

44

Chapter Twelve

Step Ten

47

Chapter Thirteen

Step Eleven

52

Chapter Fourteen

Step Twelve

56

Chapter Fifteen

Meeting with Clarence Snyder

59

Chapter Sixteen

What Early A.A. was really like

61

Chapter Seventeen

Notes

63

Chapter Eighteen

About the Author

64

LOVE

If I speak in human and angelic tongues but do not have love, I am a resounding gong or a clashing cymbal. And if I have the gift of prophecy and comprehend all mysteries and all knowledge; if I have all faith so as to move mountains but do not have love, I am nothing. If I give away everything I own, and if I hand my body over so that I may boast but do not have love, I gain nothing.

Love is patient, love is kind. It is not jealous, (love) is not pompous, it is not inflated, it is not rude, it does not seek its own interests, it is not quick-tempered, it does not brood over injury, it does not rejoice over wrongdoing but rejoices with the truth. It bears all things, believes all things, hopes all things, endures all things.

Love never fails. If there are prophecies, they will be brought to nothing; if tongues, they will cease; if knowledge, it will be brought to nothing. For we know partially and we prophesy partially, but when the perfect comes, the partial will pass away. When I was a child, I used to talk as a child, think as a child, reason as a child; when I became a man, I put aside childish things. At present we see indistinctly, as in a mirror, but then face to face. At present I know partially; then I shall know fully, as I am fully known. So faith, hope, love remain, these three; but the greatest of these is love. I Corinthians 13

INTRODUCTION

This program is simple but not easy. The essence of the program is putting the Word of God, Sacred Scripture, into action.
As the book of Second Timothy 3:16-17 states: "all scripture is inspired by God and profitable for teaching, for reproof, for correction and for training in righteousness, so that the man of God may be complete, equipped for every good work".

For those who need to recover from alcohol or drug abuse, who need to recover from a gambling addiction, those who wish to break the nicotine addiction, who need healing from depression, for those who have an eating disorder, and for you who suffer from a sexual or pornographic addiction, to those who need to recover from an abortion, for those who suffer from any mental, emotional, or physical malady, for those who have suffered financially due to no fault of your own, those who have lost friends and family members, and those of you who have lost your way, who need to be "restored", to be brought back to wholeness again within the body of Christ, this program is for you.

According to the Merriam-Webster Dictionary, to be recovered means "to bring back to normal position or condition". The Cambridge Dictionary states: "to get back something lost, especially health, ability, possessions, etc". All Words.Com " To regain one's good health, spirits or composure". And from WordNet, "cured, healed, recovered, freed from illness or injury; found after being lost".

Before going through the steps you must stop whatever you are doing that hinders your fellowship with God. If you need to be taken out of the environment by way of detox or rehab then you must make the move. And when you are ready to go through these steps you must do them with another person. "Where two or more are gathered together in my name, there I am in their midst". Matthew 18:20

Now it is time to ask yourself, who's the boss-you, or the problems you are facing? Have many phases of your life become unmanageable because of your problem or problems? It stands to reason that if you can't manage your life then you need someone who can. Another words, you need a new manager!

You must ask yourself the following questions: 1) What am I willing to do to get rid of the problem? 2) What am I willing to do to get rid of the effects the problem has on my life? 3) When do I want to get better to recover?

If you are willing then your new manager Jesus Christ will heal you and take care of your life.

If you feel this program is too hard or that you feel you are unworthy of God's love, listen to what Jesus is saying in Matthew 11:28-30, " Come to me, all you who labor and are burdened, and I will give you rest. Take my yoke upon you and learn from me, for I am meek and humble of heart, and you will find rest for yourselves. For my yoke is easy, and my burden light".

And from the Book of Philippians 4:13, "I can do all things through Christ who strengthens me".

Chapter One
The Christian 12 Step Recovery Program

1. I admit that I am powerless over the effects of my separation or lack of fellowship with God and that my life has become unmanageable.
2. I believe that the power of Jesus Christ, through the working of the Holy Spirit, will restore me to fellowship with God.
3. I will make a decision to turn my will and my life over to the care of God.
4. I will take a searching and fearless moral inventory of myself.
5. I will admit to God, to myself, and to another human being, the exact nature of my wrongs.
6. I will become entirely ready to have God remove all of my sins.
7. I will humbly ask Him to remove them.
8. I will make a list of all persons I have harmed, and become willing to make amends to them all.
9. I will make direct amends to such people wherever possible, except when to do so would injure them or others.
10. I will continue to take a daily personal inventory, and when I am wrong, I will try to promptly admit it.
11. I will seek through prayer and meditation to improve my contact with God, praying only for the knowledge of His will for me and the power to carry it out.

12. Having had a spiritual awakening as the result of these steps, I will try to carry this message to others and I will try to practice these principles in all of my affairs.

The first three steps are about making your peace with God.

Step One is recognizing your broken.
Step Two is about the birth of faith in you.
Step Three involves a decision to let God be in charge of your life.

Steps Four through Seven are about making peace with ourselves.

Step Four involves self-examination.
Step Five is the discipline of confession.
Step Six is an inner transformation sometimes called repentance.
Step Seven involves the transformation or purification of your character.

Steps Eight through Ten are about peace with others.

Step Eight involves examining your relationships and preparing ourselves to make amends.

Step Nine is the discipline of making amends.

Step Ten is about maintaining progress in your spiritual life.

Steps Eleven and Twelve help us keep the peace we have established.

Step Eleven involves the spiritual disciplines of prayer and meditation.

Step Twelve is about ministry.

Chapter Two
The Journey

I know of many people who became healed of addictions by the time they reached the fourth step. However, for most, even taking the first step was a process. And it always consisted of something that we could do to help alleviate the problem. Some of us tried exercise, yoga, meditation, seeking spiritual gurus, running, health food, individual and group therapy, and unfortunately for many, they regulate their lives around attending meetings that go on for many years that are only supposed to be a temporary help.

For myself, I used all of these and I had relief for short periods of time. Then, in 1981, after suffering from a long bout of depression, I was taken through these steps by a man who literally saved my life.

Andy A. noticed that I was suffering and he told me that if I wanted help he could take me through a 12 Step Program as it was administered from its beginning. He told me he was taken through the steps by a woman who was taken through them by Clarence Snyder, who was one of the original members of A.A.

Andy and I would meet a couple of times a week. When we got to the second step he asked me if I believed in God and who or what was my idea of God. I told him that I believed God was an energy force and we could tap into this energy through meditation. This energy would then help us to overcome any problem or situation.

Andy then asked me if he could share his God with me and I agreed. He took out a picture of Jesus and handed it to me. At once, a chill went down my spine and I said; " I had a sneaky suspicion about this guy".

During my journey through the steps, I was healed of my depression along with other physical and mental ailments.

And most importantly, I developed a thirst for God and His Word, and I wanted to give others the same help I had received.

My Spiritual Journey actually began months before my meetings with Andy. I was in a VA hospital in Manhattan, NY and I was so angry I hadn't spoken to anyone for weeks and I was coming up on a discharge date when the head psychiatrist of the hospital decided to put me on a drug that would help me. He told me the drug would be available that evening at the nurse's station. I kept going to the station all evening and they kept telling me they didn't have it. Finally, after a raging mad encounter with a nurse, I went back to my room on the thirteenth floor and looked out the window at the sky and said; "God, please help me".

I was able to fall asleep that night with a peace I had never known.

The next day I was smiling and talking so much that every patient was walking up to me and shaking my hand.

The head psychiatrist heard of this and rushed to see me.
He also shook my hand and said; " I see the drug is working". I said; " I never took the drug, they never had it ready". Well, he looked at me like he saw a ghost and just walked away.

After my discharge from the hospital, I stayed close to many people in A.A. some of whom would always come into the hospital to give talks. Especially men like Benny J. and Gene W.

But it was only after I was taken through the steps that I felt I had something that could really help people.

I could now help people without thinking it was the great I am who was helping them, but I could help them find the actual "I Am", who would help them.

Now, after decades of time with my new helper, healer, savior, Jesus Christ, I love Him now more than ever.

My spiritual journey took me to many places, like preaching with a Bible on a microphone on 42nd street in Manhattan, and watching the Holy Spirit work by bringing many hurting people who just wanted prayer.

I read all kinds of Christian books, listened to only Christian music, and Christian talk radio. I read the Bible in various versions, I took Bible courses, I conducted Bible studies in hospitals and in Church. I attended numerous Christian retreats. I played the part of Jesus Christ in an off-broadway play. I put the steps on a website, I made a CD and published "A Christian 12 Step Recovery Program" along with " A How to Guide for Administering the Steps".

After being witnessed to by a dear fellow employee shortly after 9/11, I began another journey back to the faith of my youth.

I became active in the pro-life movement.

I marched in Washington D.C. and St. Augustine, Fl. I pray outside of abortion clinics in New Jersey, Florida, and Pennsylvania. I drove a pro-life truck in Manhattan and the Jersey shore.

And I became healed of the abortions that I had played a role in by providing the insurance for by attending a Rachel's Vineyard weekend retreat.

My journey through the steps has been the most rewarding spiritual exercise for me. My life has always been exciting, non-boring.

I always have another book to read or to write, another Bible book to study another person who needs prayer, another person who needs to hear the about the only person in this life who is the "Way, the

Truth, and the Life". And the only person who can lead them to His Church.

I have been blessed beyond measure.
I am truly grateful for every breath I take. For everything God has given me the good along with the bad because I know for sure that God makes all things work for good for those who love Him who are called according to His purpose. Romans 8:28

"But as it is written, eye had not seen, nor ear heard, neither have entered into the heart of man, the things which God had prepared for them that love Him". I Corinthians 2:9

Chapter Three
Step One

I admit that I am powerless over the effects of my separation or lack of fellowship with God and that my life has become unmanageable.

What is meant by being powerless? Does it mean there is nothing we can do with our own power? No amount of money, or wishing or hoping, no amount of secular programs or medications can alleviate the effects of our separation or lack of fellowship with God.

"For the flesh has desires against the spirit, and the spirit against the flesh; these are opposed to each other, so that you may not do what you want.." Galatians 5:17

But praise God, there is One who can help us!

The Apostle Paul tells us in the Book of Romans 7:15,17,24-25. "What I do, I do not understand. For I do not do what I want, but I do what I hate. I know nothing good lives in me, that is, in my sinful nature.

For I have the desire to do what is good, but I cannot carry it out. Miserable one that I am! Who will deliver me? Thanks be to God through Jesus Christ our Lord".

Step One

Please note the word (through), because it is Jesus Christ who is going to get you through the steps.

What has caused this separation from God? The Book of Isaiah tells us, 59:2, "But your iniquities have made a separation between you and your God, and your sins have hidden His face from you, so that He does not hear".

This separation or lack of fellowship with God causes a sense of emptiness inside that we desire to fill so that we can feel better. We try to fill this empty feeling with excessive drinking, drugging, gambling, pornography, overeating, and many substitute money and material items as their god. These excesses can lead to illness and sometimes death. As someone once said; "the temporary or seemingly good is often the deadly enemy of the permanent best".

Ever since our creation, we have been rebelling against God.

Right before God destroyed the earth by a flood of water He said; "...how great was man's wickedness on earth, and how no desire that his heart conceived was ever anything but evil". Genesis 6:5

Step One

What we all need is a clean heart. A heart that accepts God for who He is, and a heart that desires to be filled on a daily basis, not of worldly things or desires but to be filled with the Holy Spirit of God. Pray this Psalm, "Create in me a clean heart, O God; and renew a right spirit within me". Psalm 51:10

Before going on to the next step you must ask yourself the following questions. Do you believe that no human power can relieve your problem and that God can and will if you seek Him?

Do you admit that you are powerless over your problems and they have made your life unmanageable?

Do you believe you have acted in a manner that is not very sane?

What are you willing to do to get well?

When do you want to get well?

Chapter Four
Step Two

I believe that the power of Jesus Christ, through the working of the Holy Spirit, will restore me to fellowship with God.

Believers in Jesus come to believe in Him in a variety of ways. For some it is sudden like a flash of light that opened their heart and eyes. "The Lord opened the eyes of the blind: the Lord raised them that are bowed down". Psalm 146:8

Many people already had a belief in Jesus before trying the steps but they may not have been able to see Him working in their lives or they didn't have a close personal relationship with Him.

And some found Jesus in the steps. Many can point to the exact step where they came to believe. And some came to believe through the overall experience.

Those who believed in Jesus and went astray either before the steps or afterwards, God speaks to them, " I will heal their backsliding, I will love them freely: for my anger is turned away from them". Hosea 14:4

Step Two

God created us with free will. Because of this freedom we are able to choose what we want in this life. Some of us choose life and some choose death. This has been the case ever since we were created by God. However, the irony of choosing life is that even though we die to self and one day will actually experience a physical death, we live, and we live forever by way of what Jesus did for us by going to the Cross dying for our sins, rising and ascending up to heaven to show us this is available to all. "For God so loved the world, that He gave His only Son, so that whoever believes in Him, should not perish, but have eternal life". John 3:16

There are many "Musts" in the book Alcoholics Anonymous. And this program is no different. Jesus Christ is the only one on this earth or in heaven above who can heal us. We must come to believe in Him to receive our healings. He is our "Great Physician" James 5:14-18
He is our Mediator for us with God the Father: I Timothy 2:5, 2 Timothy 2:9,10

You must believe Jesus is telling the truth when He states; "I am the Way, the Truth, and the Life, no one comes to the Father, except by me". John 14:6

Chapter Five
Step Three

I will make a decision to turn my will and my life over to the care of God.

Since you made the decision that you needed to come under new management because your own way of doing things got you nowhere, you are now ready to turn your life by the use of your will over to the care of your new power and new manager Jesus Christ.

Say the following prayers: Lord Jesus, I am coming to you in all humility to ask you to guide and direct me. I realize that my life is messed up and unmanageable.

God the Father, I come to you in the name of Your Son Jesus Christ. I ask you to come into my heart. I give you my life and my will, and pray that Your perfect will be done for me today.

God, I offer myself to thee, to build me and to do with me as thou will. Relieve me of the bondage of self, that I may better do Thy will. Take away my difficulties, that victory over them may bear witness to those I may help of they power, love, and way of life. May I do they will always.

Step Three

Let us now see what God thinks about what you just did. "The Lord thy God in the midst of thee is mighty; He will save, He will rejoice over thee with joy; You will rest in His love, He will joy over thee with singing". Zephaniah 3:17

"For the Father Himself loves you, because you have loved Me, and have believed that I came out from God". John 16:27

"That I may cause those that love Me to inherit substance, and I will fill their treasures". Proverbs 8:21

"Because he has set his love upon Me, therefore will I deliver him: I will set him on high, because he hath known My Name". Psalm 91:14

"...I tell you, there will be rejoicing among the angels of God over one sinner who repents". Luke 15:10

The evil one now no longer has control over your life. He will keep trying to tempt you in various ways and may even think he has succeeded but although he may win some future battles, he has already lost the war!!!!

Step Three

There is now nothing on this earth nor in heaven above that can separate you from the love of God. Romans 8:31-39

Your spirit of fear has been removed and you now have been given a spirit of power, love, and a sound mind. 2 Timothy 1:7

You can now approach God with freedom and confidence. Ephesians 3:12. You are now a minister of reconciliation for God. 2 Corinthians 5:17-21

If you have not done so already please find a good Church and Bible study, read the Bible daily, and pray always.

"Be diligent to present yourself approved to God as a workman who does not need to be ashamed, handling accurately the Word of Truth". 2 Timothy 2:15

"Trust in the Lord with all your heart and do not lean on your own understanding. In all your ways acknowledge Him, and He will make your paths straight. Do not be wise in your own eyes; fear the Lord and turn away from evil. It will be healing to your body and refreshment to your bones". Proverbs 3:5-8

Chapter Six
Step Four

I will take a searching and fearless moral inventory of myself.

The fourth step may take several pages or may take only one. It usually depends upon how honest you are and how much you can recall.

You may read, or give the inventory to your Priest, Rabbi, Minister, trusted friend, or nobody. The important thing is that you do it before you go on to the next step.

If you have trouble doing this step say the following prayer: Jesus, I can't do this, I do not want to do this, please do it for me".

These words of Jesus from the Gospel of Matthew chapter seven are the crux of this step. "Why do you look at the speck that is in your brother's eye, but do not notice the log that is in your own eye? Or how can you say to your brother,'let me take the speck out of your eye,' and behold, the log is in your own eye? You hypocrite, first take the log out of your own eye, and then you will see clearly how to take the speck out of your brother's eye".

We must clean our own house before we can help someone else.

Step Four

Here are some scriptures to help you with this step.

"Let us examine our ways and test them, and let us return to the Lord". Lamentations 3:40

"For the Word of God is living and active and sharper than any two-edged sword, and piercing as far as the division of soul and spirit, of both joints and marrow, and able to judge the thoughts and intentions of the heart. And there is no creature hidden from His sight, but all things are open and laid bare to the eyes of Him with whom we have to do". Hebrews 4:12-13

"But prove yourselves doers of the Word, and not merely hearers who delude themselves. For if anyone is a hearer of the Word and not a doer, he is like a man who looks at his natural face in a mirror: for once he has looked at himself and gone away, he has immediately forgotten what kind of person he was. But one who looks intently at the perfect law, the law of liberty, and abides by it, not having become a forgetful hearer but an effectual doer, this man shall be blessed in what he does". James 1:22-25

Step Four

"Don't be afraid, because I am your God. I will make you strong and will help you; I will support you with My right hand that saves you". Isaiah 41:10

You must use the same categories that are in this workbook.

The "Shout Out" column is for you to write down what you are feeling while remembering each person, etc.

The categories can be overlapping, for example; you may have had a friend that you worked with and also lived with, but your "Shout Out" may be different for the person based on the circumstances.

The fourth step is more than putting down your resentments. God wants to heal all of you, not just the things that we want healed.

Step Four

Family **Friends** **Shout Out**

Step Four

People lived with	Means of Support	Shout Out

Step Four

Sex Partners	Fears & Obsessions	Shout Out

Step Four

Lies told or truths withheld **People worked with** **Shout Out**

_____
_____
_____
_____
_____
_____
_____
_____
_____
_____
_____
_____
_____
_____
_____
_____
_____
_____
_____
_____

Step Four

People you socialized with   **Shout Out**

_____

_____

_____

_____

_____

_____

_____

_____

_____

_____

_____

_____

_____

_____

_____

_____

_____

_____

_____

_____

Step Four

Resentments towards institutions   **Shout Out**

_____
_____
_____
_____
_____
_____
_____
_____
_____
_____

Somethings that nobody was to ever know   **Shout Out**

_____
_____
_____
_____
_____
_____
_____
_____
_____
_____

Step Four

Events you wished had never happened　　　　　　　　**Shout Out**

Chapter Seven
Step Five

I will admit to God, to myself and to another human being, the exact nature of my sins.

Now that you took your inventory, is there anything this "burning you", something that you never told anyone about?

Now look at your fourth step and admit if a particular sin applies to you. You do not have to go into details of each sin, that is all up to you. All is asked is that you are honest and admit your sins to yourself, and to God. It is suggested that you take this step with either a Priest, Rabbi, Minister, or Pastoral Counselor.

Here is your scripture: "If we confess our sins, He is faithful and just and will forgive us our sins and purify us from all unrighteousness". I John 1:9

Here is a list of sins to help you; self-pity, self-justification, self-importance, self-condemnation, dishonesty, impatience, resentments, false pride, jealousy, envy, laziness, procrastination, insincerity, negative thinking, immoral thinking, criticizing, fear, greed, stealing, lust, gluttony, and gossip.

Chapter Eight
Step Six

I will become entirely ready to have God remove all of my sins.

Here are your scriptures; "Be gracious to me, O God, according to Thy loving kindness; according to the greatness of Thy compassion blot out my transgressions. Wash me throughly from my iniquity, and cleanse me from my sin. Fo I know my transgressions, and my sin is ever before me. Against Thee, Thee only, I have sinned, and done what is evil in Thy sight, so that Thou are justified when You speak, and blameless when you judge". Psalm 51:1-4

"Whoever tries to keep his life will lose it, and whoever loses his life will preserve it". Luke 17:33

Now that you have admitted your sins, you need to get rid of them. These sins caused your life to be unmanageable.
You can't ask God to get rid of the things you did in your past. However, you can ask Him to get rid of the sins which caused you to act in the manner you did.

Are you ready to get rid of all your sins? Even the ones that are fun? Remember, you turned your life and will over to God in step three.

Chapter Nine
Step Seven

I will humbly ask Him to remove them.

Now you must humbly ask that your sins be removed, those that you admitted to in Step Five.

Here is your scripture: "Therefore if any man is in Christ, he is a new creature: the old things are passed away; behold, all things made new". II Corinthians 5:17

Say the following prayers; I humbly ask you oh Lord, to remove my shortcomings and forgive me of my sins and ask in all humility that you will remove my sins because I am one of your children and I truly believe. My sins are: (read the list you admitted to in step five). Thank You Jesus, thank You Jesus, thank You Jesus, Amen, Amen, Amen.

My creator, I am now willing that you have all of me, good and bad. I thank you for removing from me every sin that stood in the way of my usefulness to You and my fellows. Grant me strength, as I go out from here to do Your bidding. Praise God thank You Jesus, praise God thank You Jesus, praise God thank You Jesus. Amen

Chapter Ten
Step Eight

I will make a list of all persons I have harmed, and become willing to make amends to them all.

Now go back to your fourth step and look for all the people you have harmed starting with yourself. Then write down next to them what sin or sins were operating in your relationship with them. You have the list of sins you admitted to in your fifth step.

You must become willing to make amends to all the people on your list. If there is a certain person or persons in whom you are not willing to make amends, you must pray for them and ask God for the willingness. Being "willing" is the key to this step.

Here are your scriptures: "Therefore, if you are offering your gift at the altar and there remember that your brother has something against you, leave your gift there in front of the altar. First go and be reconciled to your brother; then come and offer your gift".
Matthew 5:23-24
"When you stand to pray, forgive anyone against whom you have a grievance, so that your heavenly Father may in turn forgive you your transgressions". Mark 11:25

Step Eight

Yourself	Sins	Family	Sins	Friends	Sins

Step Eight

Acquaintances	Sins	Employers & Institutions	Sins

Chapter Eleven
Step Nine

I will make direct amends to such people wherever possible, except when to do so would injure them or others.

Go over all the people or institutions on your eight step list. All amends that are possible must be made.

This is the step that separates the men from the boys, (or women from the girls) and the amount of finished amends will have a direct impact on how you recover and stay recovered.

If at all possible, the amends must be done directly to the person or institution, no phone calls, or letters. An important part of the healing power in this step, is when you take responsibility for your actions.

Whether the person harmed you (real or imagined) is not important. You are the person who needs to get well.

There are some reasons why an amends cannot be made directly in person; 1) the person is dead-pray to God for forgiveness. 2) You owe more money than you can pay back at the present time. Then try to pay small amounts until the debt or robbery is paid off.

Step Nine

3) the person lives too far away and you have no means to get to them-pray to God for forgiveness, but keep the person on your list for the day may come when you can go to them. 4) making amends would harm the person. If you do not think you are spiritually fit to make the amends then do not attempt it. Pray about it, talk to a spiritual director, Priest, Rabbi, Minister, etc
These type of situations do not prevent you from going further in the steps.

This step is one of the most sensitive and difficult steps. But always remember, the willingness to make an amends is always the hardest hurdle to overcome.

For us to take full responsibility for our actions is the key. Always keep in mind that we are trying to right a wrong. We are not trying to make someone understand us, our behavior, our disease, etc. Placing any responsibility on the other person omits the amends. And never give an excuse such as "I was too drunk, or I was too depressed, but surprise I am not that way anymore! And of course never give the reason for the amends as being in a program or a book you read suggests it. And never plead for forgiveness. Whether the person forgives you or not is their problem not yours.

Step Nine

The following three things must be done before venturing out on any amends. 1) Make sure the person or others will not be harmed by your amends. 2) Talk to someone about the amends because what comes to us alone may be our own rationalizations or wishful thinking. 3) Say the following prayer: Lord, make me a channel of Thy peace- that where there is hatred, I may bring love-that where there is wrong, I may bring the spirit of forgiveness-that where there is discord, I may bring harmony-that where there is error, I may bring truth-that where there is doubt, I may bring faith, that where there is despair, I may bring hope-that where there are shadows, I may bring light-that where there is sadness, I may bring joy. Lord, grant that I may seek rather to comfort than to be comforted, to understand, than to be understood-to love, than to be loved. For it is by self-forgetting that one finds. It is by forgiving that one is forgiven. It is by dying that one awakens to eternal life. Saint Francis of Assisi

"Fools mock at making amends for sin, but goodwill is found among the upright. Each heart know its own bitterness, and no one else can share its joy. The house of the wicked will be destroyed, but the tent of the upright will flourish. There is a way that seems right to a man, but in the end it leads to death". Proverbs 14:9-12

Chapter Twelve
Step Ten

I will continue to take a daily inventory, and when I am wrong, I will try to promptly admit it.

Paul tells us in the Book of Romans 12:17-19, "Do not repay anyone evil for evil. Be careful to do what is right in the eyes of everybody. If it is possible, as far as it depends on you, live at peace with everyone. Do not take revenge, my friends, but leave room for God's wrath, for it is written: 'It is mine to avenge; I will repay', says the Lord".

"What shall we say then? Shall we continue in sin, that grace may abound? God forbid. How shall we, that are dead to sin, live any longer therein? Romans 6:1-2

"Reckon yourselves to be dead indeed unto sin, but alive unto God through Jesus Christ our Lord. Let not sin therefore reign in your mortal body, that you should obey it in the lusts thereof". Romans 6:11-12

"Stand fast therefore in the liberty wherewith Christ has made us free, and be not entangled again with the yoke of bondage". " I say then, walk in the Spirit, and you will not fulfill the lusts of the flesh". Galatians 5:1, 16

Step Ten

"But the fruit of the Spirit is love, joy, peace, long suffering, gentleness, goodness, faith, meekness, temperance: against such there is no law. And they that are Christ's have crucified the flesh with the affections and lusts. If we live in the Spirit, let us also walk in the Spirit". Galatians 5:22-25

"Put on the whole armor of God that you may be able to stand against the wiles of the devil. For we wrestle not against flesh and blood, but against principalities, against powers, against the rulers of the darkness of this world, against spiritual wickedness in high places. Wherefore take unto you the whole armor of God, that ye may be able to withstand in the evil day, and having done all, to stand. Stand therefore, having your loins girt about with truth, and having on the breastplate of righteousness; and your feet shod with the preparation of the gospel of peace; above all, taking the shield of faith, wherewith ye shall be able to quench all the fiery darts of the wicked. And take the helmet of salvation, and the sword of the Spirit, which is the Word of God: praying always with all prayer and supplication in the Spirit, and watching thereunto with all perseverance and supplication for all saints;" Ephesians 6:11-18

Step Ten

"For by grace you have been saved through faith; and that not of yourselves, it is the gift of God; not as a result of works so that no one may boast. For we are His workmanship, created in Christ Jesus for good works, which God prepared beforehand so that we would walk in them". Ephesians 2:8-10

"Therefore as you have received Christ Jesus the Lord, so walk in Him, having been firmly rooted and now being built up in Him and established in your faith, just as you were instructed, and overflowing with gratitude. See to it that no one takes you captive through philosophy and empty deception, according to the tradition of men, according to the elementary principles of the world, rather than according to Christ. For in Him all the fullness of Deity dwells in bodily form, and in HIm you have been made complete, and He is the head over all rule and authority; Let no one keep defrauding you of your prize by delighting in self-abasement and the worship of the angels, taking his stand on visions he has seen, inflated without cause by his fleshly mind", Colossians 2:6-9

Step Ten

"But I say to you, love your enemies, bless them that curse you, do good to them that hate you, and pray for those who despitefully use you, and persecute you; that you may be the children of your heavenly Father; for He makes His sun to rise on the evil and on the good, and sends rain on the just and on the unjust". Matthew 5:44-45

Practice taking your personal inventory nightly. Did you harm anyone? Did you do something wrong? Then ask God for forgiveness, and by His Grace He will forgive you, clean slate.

If you were wrong, try to promptly admit it. Try to deal with your life by using the Four Absolutes; Absolute Love, Absolute Honesty, Absolute Unselfishness, Absolute Purity. Did you act out of love? Were you honest? Were your motives pure?

Remember, we still have free will and the right to choose. We can bring back any of our sins that God had healed us of in the Seventh Step. The purpose of Step Ten is to recognize them quickly before they steamroll into more sins.

Here is a Daily Inventory List to help you in achieving your goal of having good relationships.

Step Ten

DAILY INVENTORY

Liability	Asset
Self-Pity	Self-Forgetfulness
Self-Justification	Humility
Self-Importance	Modesty
Self-Condemnation	Self-Valuation
Dishonesty	Honesty
Impatience	Patience
Hate	Love
Resentment	Forgiveness
False Pride	Simplicity
Jealousy	Trust
Envy	Generosity
Laziness	Activity
Procrastination	Promptness
Insincerity	Straight Forwardness
Negative Thinking	Positive Thinking
Vulgar, Immoral	Spiritual
Fear	Courage
Criticizing	Look for the good
Trashy Thinking	Clean Thinking

Chapter Thirteen
Step Eleven

I will seek through prayer and meditation to improve my conscious contact with God. Praying for the knowledge of His will and for His power to carry it out.

Prayer is talking to Go. Meditation is listening to Him. Pray, go to Church, and read the Bible. Get to know the Word of God and the teachings of His Church so you can better understand them.

Learn to pray constantly, not just once or twice a day. God want to be your every day, every moment, manager. In 1981 I was told by the man who took me through these steps to say "Praise God thank You Jesus" all the time, in good times and bad, when working, when doing anything. And I have continued saying this multiple times throughout the day over all these years. "...enter into His gates with thanksgiving and into His courts with praise: be thankful unto Him, and bless His Name". Psalm 100:4

Reading a Psalm every day is the one of the best ways to have gratitude in your heart, along with prayer and praise on your lips.

I also recommend a very powerful way to pray and meditate over Scripture, "Lectio Divina". Several years ago I found the Holy Rosary to also be a great form of meditation.

Step Eleven

How do you pray? Many people pray but some do not know the God of creation who made all things and will return again to earth in glory. At this time in your journey through the steps you should have a good understanding of God and His miracle working power.

A prayer that helped me in 1981 was the Serenity Prayer, I had to say this constantly throughout the day in order to do anything or be with anyone.

"Let the words of my mouth, and the meditations of my heart be acceptable in Thy sight, O Lord, my strength and my redeemer". Psalm 19:14

"Thy Word have I hidden in my heart that I may not sin against Thee". Psalm 119:11

"Delight yourself also in the Lord; and He shall give you the desires of your heart". Psalm 37:4

If you do not have a Bible you need to get one ASAP. And after you do, look up from the Book of Colossians 3:16-17

Step Eleven

Here is a prayer I found, but I no not know who the author is.

Touch me Lord like You have so many times before

I feel Your warmth surround me, I want even more!

A vision of Your love vibrates my very soul

I gave you my life, You're in total control.

Now I've seen all the Joy that I've missed

On this point I'll be Your eternal witness.

Your Holy Spirit gives me new wisdom

Your blood, has given me my freedom.

I'm no longer controlled by the lusts that I've known

You've helped me recover the bad seeds that I've sown.

My will, my strength depends on thee

Your loving grace has set my soul free.

As I pray this prayer to You, my love

I feel Your Spirit descending like a dove.

I praise the One who takes time to care

I claim Your promise, You'll always be there.

Oh Lord, when I think of what You have done

All my lost battles that You have won.

I can't wait to be together with You

Spending eternity in Your world made new.

Thank You for this time we spend

Thank You for being my eternal friend.

Step Eleven

When I look at the wondrous works of thee

What am I Lord, that You are mindful of me?

Yet I feel Your love inside

Like roaring waves at high tide.

You wrap me so tight with Your love

I feel safe inside Your heavenly glove.

Your blood, Oh Lord, cleanses me of sin

Only by Your grace shall I remain within.

I promise to keep my eyes on You

And You've promised to see me through.

Lord, as I carry on my day

Help me to love, honor and obey.

Thank You, Lord, for listening to me again

Be with me always, Jesus, I love You, Amen

Pray, Meditate, and Seek the guidance of God. Let His will, not yours, be done!

Chapter Fourteen
Step Twelve

Having had a spiritual awakening as the result of these steps, I will try to carry this message to others and I will try to practice these principles in all of my affairs.

This program is not dependent upon winning friends and influencing people. If a person balks, or begins to ask too many questions, they are not ready. However, if you believe that a person is ready to go through these steps then you must not hesitate.

You are now a minister of reconciliation. You are not to be used as a place for someone to be always dumping their garbage, giving extensive drunkalogs, or psychobabble. You are in charge so keep the person focused on the particular step you are doing. It is your responsibility to give this message to others as you have received it, not changed, watered down, or how others may want to do them.

We are not to judge a person's heart, but to use the wisdom of God to discern: 1) Is the person ready to go through the steps? 2) What step is the person on? 3) What help you can give the person with each step. 4) And most important of all is to know when to "let go" of the person and "let God" work through them so they can help others.

Step Twelve

Whenever we are witnessing, disciplining, twelve stepping, we must do it in the Spirit and Wisdom of God. We must use His Power and Guidance, or the "fruit" will be ours and not His. The results will be from our doing and not from the Heart of God. Therefore, never rush anyone through the steps, but let the Hand of God take you and the person you are working with one step at a time.

Here are the Four Phases to the Steps: Step One: Admission, Steps Two-Seven: Submission, Steps Eight and Nine: Restitution, Steps Ten-Twelve: The Living Steps, construction and maintenance.

A Spiritual Awakening is the "Result" of working, doing, and living, "All" of the Twelve Steps; then you have a message to carry to others. There is no message unless you have done the first nine steps and you are living in the last three.

There is no easier softer way, this is it. This is the program of recovery.

You can and do recover. You don't have to stay sick. You can and do get well!!

Step Twelve

Recovery is letting God do for you what you cannot do for yourself. It is the simple but challenging process of daily seeking God's will for your life instead of demanding to go your own way.

Without God, there is no recovery, only disappointing substitutions and repeated failure. God wants to heal your brokenness and set you on the path toward wholeness.

"Brethren, if a man is overtaken in any trespass, you who are spiritual should restore him in a spirit of gentleness. Look to yourself, lest you too be tempted". Galatians 6:1

"The things which you have heard from me in the presence of many witnesses, entrust these to faithful men who will be able to teach others also". 2 Timothy 2:2

Chapter Fifteen
Meeting with Clarence Snyder

In the early 1980's I attended a retreat in upstate New York. The retreat was run by the late Clarence Snyder. Clarence was one of the original members of A.A. You will find his name in the book Dr. Bob and the Good Old-Timers, however, very little is mentioned about him in other A.A. literature.

I was told by Clarence that the God I came to believe in while doing the Twelve Steps was the God of A.A. and His Name is Jesus Christ.

In his speech, Clarence told us they would go into hospitals and find new recruits because they had learned that in order to keep their lives sober, they had to give it away to others. What they gave away was the "great commission" given by Jesus, "Go therefore and make disciples of all the nations, baptizing them in the name of the Father and the Son and the Holy Spirit, teaching them to observe all that I commanded you; and lo, I am with you always, even to the end of the age". Matthew 28:19-20

They would have men get out of their hospital beds and get them on their knees to pray.

Meeting with Clarence Snyder

Clarence said he broke away from A.A. after General World Services in Manhattan, New York started to change the language of the program. He was deeply disturbed when they added the phrase "God as we understood Him". along with the Twelfth Step omitting the phrase "carrying this message to other", and replacing it with "carrying the message to alcoholics".

He also stated that Bill Wilson's spiritual experience was with Jesus Christ.

Even though Clarence did not agree with the "watering down" of the program by Bill W. and Dr. Bob, he had no disparaging remarks to say about them.

Until his death, Clarence Snyder held retreats all over, letting the world know what early A.A. was really like.

It was a Jewish Woman who met Clarence on one of his retreats and he took her through this Christian 12 Step Recovery Program , she then took Andy A. through the steps, and it was Andy A. who took me through them.

Chapter Sixteen
What early A. A. was really like

You won't learn this in A.A.'s basic text today or in its meetings. But the simplicity of early A.A. will really astound you and attract!

There usually was hospitalization or at least medical help to save the newcomer's life. Only the Bible was allowed in the room. Recovered drunks visited the patient and told their success stories. Yes, "Recovered", the early members always said they were "Recovered" and also gave their full names so they would be able to be contacted by those in need. Two questions were asked of the patients in the hospital. Do you believe in God? Are you willing to get down on your knees and pray?

After hospitalization many were too sick to venture far; so they lived with the Smiths and others in Akron, Ohio homes. Here they learned what a loving God had made available where they had daily quiet time along with Bible study, prayer, devotional readings, guidance, and discussions of Anne Smith's Journal. They learned to take these back into their own homes.

Meetings were once a week. No drunkalogs, no whining, no psychobabble, just prayer, scripture reading, devotional reading from the Upper Room or similar devotionals and of course quiet times.

What early A.A. was really like

Newcomers surrendered their addictions in a prayer session resembling that in the Book of James 5:14-16
The elders prayed with them for healing and that the person would subsequently devote themselves to live according to God's will.

Dr. Bob gave sessions on a moral inventory, adherence to the four absolutes, confession, prayer to have sins removed and plans for restitution. Did it work? You bet it did. 75% recovered in Akron, soon 93% were recovering in Cleveland. Compare these figures to the 1% that most secular rehabs report today.

They always had announcements about new people in hospitals.

Chapter Seventeen
Notes

Here are some pages of books and other literature from the early days.

As Bill Sees It, page 67, A.A. Comes of Age pages 39 and 231-232
Dr. Bob and Good Old Timers pages 96-97,71,136,139-140,151,178,220,and pages 310-311.

The Language of the Heart, pages 298 and 177-178,356-357
Pass It On, pages 147, 169,171-172 and 197

The website for the ministry is www.recoveredthroughchrist.com
You can find an audio recording of the entire program at
www.godtube.com/themessagecarrier
You can find my books at
www.lulu.com/rtcm49

All scripture quotations are taken from the following Bibles in such a way so that there is no infringement on the copyrights.
The New American Bible, the New American Standard Version, the King James Version, the New King James Version.

Chapter Eighteen
About the Author

I was born in Paterson, New Jersey. My father was a factory worker and my mother was a saleswoman. They worked together and achieved the American Dream.

My father was my best friend. Every Sunday he would take me to Eastside Park or Garret Mountain to play baseball. We would often wrestle on the living room floor while watching sports. But the most important thing my father showed me was "forgiveness". He never held a grudge. His good nature was noted by his union and they made him shop steward.

At 3 a.m. in the morning on the 19th of March 1963, I was awakened by the screams of my mother. I got up and went by her and saw she was crying over the phone to someone and at the sametime was stomping her feet on the floor (we rented out the first floor to an Registered Nurse). I then walked by the bathroom and saw my father throwing up blood in the toilet. It appeared the toilet was overflowing with his blood. He then walked out to the kitchen and sat down on one of the kitchen chairs. My mother was standing by him. He asked her for a drink of water. As soon as she turned around to the sink to get the water, he began throwing up again, and subsequently, fell off the chair and died in his own blood on the kitchen floor, to my mother, sister, and me, it was the most horrible think we had ever seen.

About the author

I know it was the most horrible and saddest thing that anyone of us would see for the rest of our lives. When my father fell off the chair I was at the back door about to head downstairs to get the nurse, I remember seeing my sister's nightgown covered in her father's blood because she tried to stop him falling.

I do not know who called him or how he got there but very soon, Father Joe C. was sitting on the couch with his arms around my mother who could not stop crying hysterically. I firmly believe this good Priest who sat with my mother for hours was sent by God to help save her because I was witnessing the loss of both parents. My mother never remarried and lived to be 88 yrs. Old and enjoyed an abundant life with her children, grandchildren and great grandchild. If anyone on this earth ever reminded me of Mother Mary it was my mother.

Prior to this tragedy, I was Mr. Popularity in school. I would learn all the new dances and would get in front of the class and sing songs to them. But after losing my best friend I became an angry 13 yr. Old. How could this happen? So sudden with no warning? How could my best friend not be there for me anymore? I felt lost, alone, and very angry. This anger would stay with me for twenty more years.

About the author

One day, after a friend of mine died suddenly, I found myself crying uncontrollably. I was crying everywhere, and it seemed like I was crying for several weeks, when suddenly I realized that all of my crying was not just for my friend, but I was finally crying over the death of my father. Father Joe C. had seen this in me at my father's funeral and he took me outside and said "now is the time to cry, that it will be good for you", but I couldn't.

This time of crying was when Andy A. saw there was something wrong with me and took me through these steps and saved my life.

Not put the focus back on yourself and how you can allow Jesus Christ to get you through the steps because He is the Author and Finisher of our Faith!

www.ingramcontent.com/pod-product-compliance
Lightning Source LLC
Chambersburg PA
CBHW081349040426
42450CB00015B/3358